AF544659

Brant Point

The University Press
of New England

Sponsoring Institutions:
Brandeis University
Clark University
Dartmouth College
University of New Hampshire
University of Rhode Island
University of Vermont

For Jean and Ronny,
at the apex of their journey
in a generous cause!
—Alex

Plainfield
18 April 1976

Brant Point

Poems by Alexander Laing

Published for Dartmouth College by
The University Press of New England
Hanover, New Hampshire 1975

Library of Congress Catalogue Card Number 75-10877

International Standard Book Number 0-87451-114-3 Clothbound

International Standard Book Number 0-87451-115-1 Paperbound

Printed in the United States of America

ACKNOWLEDGMENTS

The Atlantic Monthly "Condottière"
The Boston Globe "Lines for an Inauguration: 20 January 1973"
The Carleton Miscellany "Brant Point"; "Candace"
Counter/Measures "A Prayer for his Friend in the Hospital"
Granite "High Suttee"; "The Parrot"
Harper's "Parents, Beware"
The Humanist "This Day"; "The Recycling of Jane"
Kayak "Memory, Quick Dolphin"
The Nation "Graffito"; "Know-How"; "Man in the Street: Mexico"; "Virtuous Pagan"; "Where Man Most Was"; "The Wildfire"
The New York Quarterly "The Trout"
Northern Lights "Deep Meadow"; "Great Society"
The New Yorker "David Today"; "Original Sin"; "Primavera"
Poetry "Locked Antlers"
The Quest "Parley in the Middle Ground"
The Saturday Review "Adventurer, Lexington Avenue Express"; "Bright Heraclitus"; "The Good Treason"; "The Hot Gate"; "Iron Mirror"; "March"; "Occurrence in October"
The Sewanee Review "Ortelius"
Vanity Fair "Peregrine"

NOTE: Most of these poems are recent. Nine earlier ones have been identified by two dates—of their origin and of their completion.

TO RONI, THIS DAY

Contents

This Day

But for your quicker looking, they would not be there:
toadstool, scarlet and ocher—umber leaf
charted with river systems—a clothes-pin swallow
clipped to his telephone wire.
                                        Where your eyes seek
a doe grows out of the dusk to meet your seeking.

You run: the tilted skitter of your running
tightens my throat, and the floor of the pine wood quickens
with small discoveries hidden until this day.

Under dark branches, where there was nothing at all,
your hand flicks mine and the world leafs open in autumn.

•1•

The Wildfire

Deep Dark

in my deep dark
the folded colors
cluster
ocher   ivory   mauve

half a hair wide
under thin plates of horn
my brooks of crimson
foam
in their braided millions
through this deep dark
where the wild bonesticks
twist
on opal pivots
my armature
and the long tidal ripple
stirs
in the midst of all
while ardent motes
scored with tomorrow's pattern
hanker
for present joy
in my deep dark

Occurrence in October

Chinking on hardpan, my long shovel
levels to hoist deep topsoil to the barrow—
and with it, an oddity, bump-skinned.
    A truffle, maybe?
Small, black brightness glints. I kneel
as my truffle opens a wart that becomes an eye,
lifts a minutely-fingered
outraged hand against the light's intrusion.
What have I done? What am I to do?
As I cup the sodden limpness of your sleep
in this blood-raveled hand, I give you
quick April. Your galvanic leap
returns you to October.
    What are we to do?
Stumbling, I drive the blade
in rumpled soil,
place you as far as you were below the surface.
You lunge, you scrabble at the crumbling walls.
    As I sift well-meant earth
you leap, and leap more wildly, shaking it off.
Now you are hidden, but the fresh earth trembles.
Now you are wholly buried.
    What have I done?

Abishag

> —and let her lie in thy
> bosom, that my lord the king
> may get heat.
> —I Kings: 1

Death prowls at the foot of my bed.
The girl lies at my heart.
Running to rumor now
a wild storm wanes.
Go away, go away death
this one more time.

The kestrel slicing air
labors his harsh wing.
The deeper black of light
creases in strips the sky.
Go away, go away death
this one more time.

What brushes the soles of my feet?
The girl stirs at my heart
thigh moving over my thigh
breast finding my mouth.
Love in the morning air
this one more time.

Ortelius

I walked to the edge of his life and stared over the edge
past hair's-breadth latitudes that hooped his globe—
spied him with elbows on a planet-gemmed
arc of the ecliptic: Abraham Ortel
comparing sea cards, shuffle, glance, and shuffle,
from Doar to Mozambique—the vellum beaches
footing steep glades that groove their ways uphill
toward slippery Prester John. Sun on wet sand
picks out no hop-prints of the monoped,
no mastiff ants, no cyclops or four-eyed men,
that one expects to find. Abraham Ortel
walking his spread dividers down the rim
of Arabia Felix; telling Strabo off;
giving great Ptolemy—where news runs thin
beyond the portolans—his strictest due,
no gulfs for habit's sake. Light nicks the sea,
dazzles. He nods. His quick engraver sends
gay monsters rollicking down these longitudes
to rout our ancient dread. Echoes of joy
strike cauldron and icicle in the twist of time,
in the great lunge of his mind across geography.

The Wildfire

Take this flame in your hands.
Yes, it will sear.
Shape it until it stands
cool as a spire.

Turn it. Study the flaws.
Blow from heart's heat
new spiculate fire. Cause
the wounds to shut.

Then, as your hurts abate,
let the skin tauten.
Needle the blebs and wait.
Your scars will whiten.

When the Tall Girl Falls

Hang up philosophy!
Unless philosophy
can make a Juliet.
—R & J III:56

Beauty? She's trapped in the observing eye.
When the tall girl falls in the forest she makes no sound
unless I am there to hear her. Then she whispers
soft enticements from the rustling ground—
or so I like to think as I think about her
imaged upon the retina's nervy wall
beautiful in the eye of a beholder
whose inward ear provides her haunting call.

Virtuous Pagan

A Last View of Professor Emeritus
J. M. M. in the Stacks
of the College Library

Huge, from this ruinous Platonic cave,
his pagan shadow haunts the river fog–
and there! Reed-pierced Sebastian, hung by the heels,
his Christian, lower image under stands.

Flame gnaws its last of wick. The great head stares,
cave-caught. The mist is lifting. These are books–
or trees?–and this tiled alley, a trout stream.
A cave of books–book-world, so like a cave.
The delicate spines of dryads everywhere.
Angels? The sweet girls, beautiful as trout,
drift down the tiers of books. Reach! Reach! The mist again.

This mind, once pickerel-swift and pickerel-still,
hung on its mucous film in the fluid cave
waiting an opening in murky thought
to dart the spoon-snout ruthlessness of "Why?"–
tearing away the soft assumption-weed.

Clear wars of conscience! Stack lights like planets turning
ring the corona of his puzzled head.
All the great causes, shut in covers, swirl
until, across our pale, fluorescent days,
light beyond light of his vast shadow falls
to measure us, who pause, against one ghost.

1953–1959

A Prayer for his Friend in the Hospital

For Ramon Guthrie

Dear God, I can't believe you're there,
but—on the off chance that you are—
I loft you this agnostic prayer.

Dart from your fierce, nucleic star,
dear God, your most abrasive jest.
Send me the worst you have to send.

But he deserves your shining best,
your Ramon, my beloved friend.

I've never figured how you play—
so, if you play it life for life,
play it your own sardonic way:
save him beneath the healing knife.

and the friends
staring wordless intensities
of their concern
he was wonderful   just wonderful
what luck to have had him at all
boxed wonder   trundled
on solemn wheels
into mirage

and the friends
with lips twisting
she'll find someone   a year maybe
year of bivouacs in a cold
desert of sheets   rimmed by mirage

and the friends
fumbling quick clutches
at her hand
so sweet and brave
someone will find her   someone

this one-owner girl
clean   a real bargain
almost no rust

Cactus at Comanjilla

from
dying rock
idiot life
pushes a
bristly
paddle
to dare
the smash of the sun

Deep Meadow

the fawn is so new
we see the grass tips stirring
but not yet the fawn

your quick spring
green drown
of coral twigs
warm   cool
waver of this
up   down
air
frog spring
eyes under meadow ice
grape hyacinth
splitting the hard lid
of turtle winter
yours to love

To Those whose Children Take Their Own Way

what else then?

if our love
won't see them through
nothing can

we wait   knowing
time's only waste
is want of love

accurate?
to the point rather
and sad—
by internal evidence
the work of a starved boy
still guessing more than he knows
of this soprano clef
of red music.

E. W. 1887–1928

The bells are quiet on the jess.
The pounces stiffen on the screen.
What climbs the air in loneliness
is now too airy to be seen.

Late falconers who strain aloft
to catch the shimmer of her sail
see only wind that whips the croft
and cloud wrack leaning to the gale.

Was ever in the sky a bird
so swift to stoop, so sure to bind
her quarry of a soaring word
in the wild weather of the mind?

Because her prey were jewel bright
do honor when the falcon dies.
Draw gently in the mews of night
the little hood across the eyes.

•2•

His Creatures

The Monkeys

Not yet five years old, I was still puzzled
by a special tang that frequently preceded
my cousins-once-removed. It was something more
than the riding boots they should have left at Durland's.
They seemed to me enormous as they bounded
into the nursery, my father hobbling
after them, in one shoe and one slipper.
He was trying to make them take back the monkey
that they had thrust upon him in the hallway.

My father's injury was his own fault.
By hiking his nightshirt up over his head
he could turn himself into the snuffler:
a hungry beast that chased me around the nursery.
I had recently made the acquaintance of God
at Sunday school on West 91st Street
and knew whom I had to thank for the intervention
when the snuffler broke a toe on my rocking horse.

The monkey was my friend. He often came
over the windowsill on a gust of music,
hoping for pennies to hide in his pillbox hat—
with first a prudent bite to test the metal.
He never before had entered at the doorway.

My small grandmother, rigid in black satin,
put down *The Roosevelt Bears* as I slid from her lap.
I could tell that she loved my cousins once removed
by the special tone in which she clucked and scolded
as they scooped her from her rocking chair and whirled her
from one to the other as if they were dancing.
They told her this was the time they were going to do it.
They had given the organ grinder a handsome fee
for his monkey's services as their consultant.
Some secret reason made it necessary.
My father said they were drunk. He gave me the monkey

and did his stumbling utmost to protect
my grandmother, who showed no liking for rescue.
While they held him, and I held the monkey,
she found her sewing basket, threaded a needle,
and told my father not to make a fuss.
It should have been done when she was a schoolgirl.

One of the cousins whispered to the monkey,
who, as I recall it, nodded briskly.
The other cousin produced a bottle,
bit out the cork, dangled the needle in it,
took a long swallow for himself, and splashed
some of the content on his handkerchief
to dab on the lobes of my grandmother's ears.
As he thrust the needle through a tab of flesh
she merely twitched, and I did all the crying.
He knotted the thread into a loop,
snipped, and repeated with the other ear.
My father was growling, but my grandmother smiled,
her mouth webbed all around with deep wrinkles.
I watched the thread loops redden until a crimson
jewel in sunlight glittered on each knot.

My grandmother walked to the mirror. Then I saw
she too was crying. The cousins-once-removed
looked at each other, suddenly panic-stricken.
She told them not to be silly. She was crying
because these were her very first earrings.
All her life she had hoped for earrings.
Happy again, they told me to bring the consultant
and persuaded him to give her a white box.
She opened it and stared at two golden monkeys,
half an inch high, except for long tails of wire
that curled up over their heads, with tiny knobs
at the tips to hold them safe in her pierced earlobes.
She kissed us all, with the biggest kiss for my father.

The Parrot

My father, whose office in a Wall Street brownstone
was hardly a jump from South Street, had a weakness
for buying oddities brought home by seamen.
One of these was a jaunty Brazilian parrot.
"Bogotá! Bogotá! Bogotá!" the bird would yell,
leering sidewise out of a gold-ringed eye,
and follow with torrents of high-sounding jabber
that nobody understood—until my father
invited the Portuguese consul and his young bride
for dinner. By telephonic prearrangement
night curtains had been drawn around the birdcage:
curtains provided to persuade the parrot
not to join in the shrill joy of our Bantam
rooster, celebrating his concupiscence
at the dark commencement of each working day.
Nothing was heard from the parrot during soup.
Regina removed the tureen. Then, with the serving
of the main course, my father winked my way.
I drew the curtains. The parrot blasted
"Bogotá! Bogotá! Bogotá!" At what followed,
the large and gently nurtured Portuguese lady
shrieked once, and fainted into the asparagus.
Later the sorrowing consul told my father
what the wicked bird had suggested to his lady,
but I could learn only his added warning—
never to buy a parrot from a sailor.

The Gulls

When I had reached years of indiscretion,
sixteen or thereabouts, my father
got me into the Huckleberry Indians—
a gentlemen's club that seemed to exist for the purpose
of strolling about on Huckleberry Island
clad in nothing but your wife's old hat
and a pair of disintegrating tennis shoes.
Prevalence of barnacles explained the latter.
As for the former, this was an era
soon after the era of hats like wedding cakes.
Ladies hid them in the guest room closet:
mementoes of their unbelievable youth—
to which, for witness, I call Charles Dana Gibson.
The first test of a new Indian's valor
was to snitch a hat. I had to make do
with one of my sister's, modestly baroque.

The only flora on Huckleberry Island
were namesake bushes—the only fauna, gulls
that often perched on a rack of 2 x 4's
erected for the preposterous cockleshells
in which the more imprudent Indians
pulled out to their stamping ground a mile offshore.
At low tide the track to Huckleberry
began with a stripe of water through green mud
where gulls had a special call, "Kee-ow! Kee-ow!"
when they swooped for killys stranded in the puddles.
As a new Indian, ravaged by self-doubt,
I had no choice but to teach myself somehow
to keep the spike-shaped, brightwork, single sculls
upright with nothing but my skittering oars
on the slap and wobble of Long Island Sound.
The gulls knew what to think: they followed, jeering,
"Gah! Gah! Gah!" My sensible father
rode out in the club launch, the *Indian,*
with a functional hat perched on each knee—
the wedding cake and his swimming Panama.

I remember the day when a gull bombed him
with a hardshell clam. The bird was merely trying
to crack it open on a ridge of rock.
Fortunately deflected by the hat,
it hit and spattered between my father's feet.
Some confusion followed on both sides.
As the gull swooped, an impulsive wallop
knocked it on its back, flapping feebly.
My father took it down to the water, soused it,
shook it awake, gave it a talking to,
and launched it on a wave. Apparently
having endured much worse in the rough career
of being a gull, the groggy bird took off.
"Valuable scavenger," my father said,
lest he be misjudged as sentimental.

The arrival at Huckleberry I best recall
came of a silly bet that I could swim
from the nearest point on shore, at turn of tide.
About a hundred yards from my destination,
as I lifted my left arm from the water,
it lifted in turn a straggle of seaweed—
or what I thought was seaweed, until its needles
jabbed me ferociously, and I saw the bubble,
red and azure, like a blown-up-coxcomb,
beside my face. I yelled, and fought off the streamers
of a Portuguese man-of-war. The Indians
strolled in the shade of their hats. An offshore breeze
blunted my cries. Then, like a rising moon,
one special hat brought comfort to the view:
half-submerged, my father's Panama.
He lolled on his back in the water. A smoke ring
rose from beyond the brim and was torn in the breeze.
My world swam back to order. A gull swooped,
crying, "Squee! Squee!" My father lifted
his sputtering cigar and answered, "Squee to you, sir."
I made it to the rocks without help.

The Turkeys

My father wore uneasily the pose
of a hard man, ready to slap tycoons
into a corner. It was pure bluff,
as he admitted, but the only way
to hold your own among the timber wolves
of Wall Street. On his fiftieth birthday
he bought two acres at the very middle
of an elegant suburb and turned gentleman farmer—
evenings and week ends. Wall Street still engaged
his more hard-hearted hours. The Property—
that was its name—at the intersection
of Pelhamdale Avenue and the Boston Post Road,
by cost accounting should have been sown to skyscrapers.
He planted it to Indian corn and spinach,
then, in the harvest season, clopped around
behind his sixteen-hander, in a Brewster
runabout giving huge crops away.

To judge by our walls, he had a reverence
for the great chromos of our early history:
the Pilgrim with a buckle to hold his hat tight,
and a wild turkey hung to his blunderbuss.
That was the one that did it. Somewhere upcounty
my father found a turkey farm and bought
four dozen day-old cheepers. Half would die,
he calculated, maybe most of them.
He also bought an authoritative tom,
rather like himself in temperament,
with a couple of hens, to make the enterprise
look right. There was a bad miscalculation:
none of the cheepers died in infancy.
My father and the tom worked up a friendship
based, one way at least, on a pocketful
of corn, scattered to bring turkeys to heel
as the Lord of the Property strolled around it
with his noisy retinue, Tom gobbler leading,

except for occasional rushes, tail spread,
wings down, to keep his flighty wives in line.

Came fall, and Pelham Manor had adolescent
turkeys perching along the wicker chairbacks
on the Manor Club porch, turkeys foraging
in gardens other folks planted to flowers.
Fresh vegetables, disbursed from willow hampers
in the boot of the runabout, failed to atone
for ravaged zinnias, or for what had happened
to the white dresses of unwary ladies
who sat down on the Manor Club's porch furniture.
Something diplomatic had to be done.
I harnessed Chester to the runabout
and sat with reins in hand, jeered at by cronies
who idled past at the wheels of glittering Packards,
while my father visited household after household
taking orders for free Thanksgiving turkeys.
What about Tom? Well–Tom was destined
for our own table, a whopping twenty pounder.
Responding to my expression, my father put on
his hard armor of the tycoon slapper.
Beasts were invented by God for man's enjoyment
while they were alive, but–mainly–after.
He was a hunter. Would he fail to eat
a succulent wild turkey if he bagged one?
He gestured toward the chromo of the Pilgrim.

A week before Thanksgiving he scanned the woodpile
for a good chopping block. I cranked the grindstone
till he had the edge he wanted on his ax.
For a couple of evenings I saw him practicing:
no wild swings–he seemed to be gripping
an invisible turkey between his knees,
head bent sidewise in his left hand,
ax held short in his right for a sudden chop.

He rigged a thick rope to hang them by their feet.
Next day was Saturday. When I drove him home
from the station, nothing was said of the coming business.
After lunch I seized a chance to vanish,
thinking he wouldn't have practiced in just that way
if he had counted on me to hold his victims.
There were some jobs a man did by himself.
From my bedroom window I saw him scattering corn
to keep his birds on the far side of a clump
of cedars between them and the block.
Not wanting to watch, I went downstairs to read
Sooner than I expected, I heard him stamp
up to the porch, and saw the ax go flying
out on the lawn. He came in, said nothing,
poured himself a Scotch, stared at the rug.
"Damn fool," he muttered presently. "Damn fool bird."
I watched him suffer over his gentle failure.
"What happened?" "Fool bird. I thought I'd kill him first.
Then the rest would be easy. Know what he did?
He came up, gobble-gobble, and stuck his head
right in my pocket. Never did that before.
Looking for corn." He turned his back abruptly.

Next day was Sunday, but he arranged somehow
for a truck stacked high with cages. Whatever happened
at the end of that journey, I never asked.
On Monday my father wanted to be met
by car, at an early train. We drove directly
to New Rochelle where he, for cash, arranged
the delivery of fifty-two prime turkeys
to various households in Pelham Manor.

Tom was a resident for some years on the Property.

The Trout

Whipping his wheel, the neighbor rode mud ridges
between the watery ruts. "Do what I can,"
he said, "if it isn't money. You know." I knew:
third year of coasting downhill from Black Friday.
June, by the calendar. Tenth day of rain,
but clouds were opening over Lake Wentworth
to let a sunset out. It flared in the doctor's
eyes, in the farmhouse doorway. "Your mother's sleeping,"
he warned me. "She sat there twenty-three hours,
till I came back. So says the student. Let her sleep."
"How is he, doctor?" "The same. Weaker.
He won't know you. Got anything for the student?"
"For him or you. I can pay him a week's worth."
"He needs it. Pay me later, or forget it
like all the rest of them." A gobbling sound
that I knew for his way of laughing jiggled his throat.
"I'm seventy-four," he said, "and it's taken me
all this time to learn to live on nothing.
So long as the store and the drugstore make deliveries—
and they still do—a doctor can live on nothing.
Nobody dares to run him out of business.
Come on. I talk too much. You know that."

The medical student, his face still lost in the gulley
of a huge textbook, gave me his chair.
My father did not know me, nor I him either.
He lay uncovered in the humid heat.
His legs, huge with edema, made me think
of duffel bags. His head, on a raveled rope
of neck, hung sidewise, its mouth open, wheezing.
"Turn him," the doctor said. "I just delivered
a baby, an hour back—my exercise
for the afternoon." I found the task obscene
trying to get a grip on the dank flesh
that had been my father. When I heaved him over
there were two bed sores you could put your fist in.

As the student dressed them I argued with my stomach.
"Spell each other tonight," the doctor counseled.
"Your mother needs her sleep." I followed him out
to the running board of his Maxwell. "How long will it be?"
I asked, and he replied, "How long do you want it
to be?" "He's done for?" "Yes, he's done for.
That's why we phoned you." "Is there anything I can do?"
He ground at the starter. "No." The engine stammered.
Then he said, "Yes. If he comes out of it,
and he just might, and be hurting, better give him
a couple of these—or three. It makes no difference."
He rummaged in his bag, stared through the bottle
at the glowing west, counted, and said, "Be careful.
Don't leave them lying around. These dozen
could kill you. Make the student go for a walk.
Your mother said he'd hardly been out of the house."

Fist in pocket, bottle in fist, I went
back to the bedside—wishing I knew the doctor
a little better, wondering what the student
was there for, if these pills were my job.
He took the borrowed money. "Can you spare it?"
The usual question, for those days, got the usual
answer, "No. Can you do without it?" "No."
Growling, he went for the walk the doctor ordered.
I sat and squeezed the bottle, wondering
how you get pills down an unconscious gullet.
I put them with the others on the bureau,
then in a drawer, then in the back of the drawer.
Later, the medical student showed me my answer:
he checked the time, balanced a pill on his finger,
and deftly thrust it into his patient's throat.
Cradling the head, he put glass to lips
and stroked the throat to the small spasm of a swallow.

I made us supper and took the first watch

till two o'clock, wondering how to endure it.
But that was needless. The memories came, chaotic.
Joel Barkalow. Name of a Barnegat guide.
Each of the three of us in his own sneakbox,
I at fourteen, hating the over-and-under
shotgun that almost kicked me into the water,
hating the killing that would make a man of me.

Plug-munching Adirondack guide, Buzz Skinner,
never spitting, drooling into the skiff
as he whispered his pinned oars through the water
of Upper Saranac—till the muskellunge struck,
smashing the skin of the lake into rainbow sparkles,
crushing my new sockdolager to fragments:
the enormous fish my father had dreamt of catching
summer after summer at Bartlett Carry.
As I staggered with my monster into the lodge
between the clicking cameras and whistles
I felt myself the captive of his pride.

Exercising Chester, the sixteen-hand
bay gelding. "A gentleman sees to his horse's comfort
before he thinks of his own." Many a midnight
when it seemed unlikely I could make the stairs
to my own bedroom, the remembered rule
sent me stumbling first into the barn
for one last forkful of straw for Chester's bedding.

The day the town fathers passed an ordinance
that could apply only to my own father:
no live chickens allowed in Pelham Manor.
They had had enough of his shrill Bantam rooster.
Our chicken coop being on the southern border,
my father bought a few square yards of Mount Vernon
and we spent a Sunday moving the coop ten feet
over the line between the jurisdictions.

After another week of shrill, pre-dawn
cock-a-doodle-doos my father journeyed
a hundred miles upstate to find his rooster
a pleasant home. We tore down the coop for kindling.
"If they'd asked me I'd have done that in the first place,"
he said when we were finished—but our fathers,
the town's and mine, had a standing misunderstanding.

And so did he and I, a clash of prides—
in one-way quarrels after I discovered
what hurt him most, the response of no response
as I in my callow dignity confronted
the Wall Street Leatherstocking, my passionate father.
He intended to train me up as his successor,
commission merchant of edible oils, Brazil nuts,
pepper: decorticated white Siam.
After two weeks of it, not a fair trial,
I stuffed some books and my foul weather gear
into a duffel bag and went to sea.

When the medical student appeared at two A. M.,
unseamanlike hour for a change of watch,
I jerked in my chair, pretended I'd been awake.
"Did the doctor tell you anything?" he asked.
"Just that he's done for. How long does that mean?"
He wrapped the rubber sock around my father's
biceps, pumped it up, and listened, scowling.
"Half a minute, maybe. Maybe a month."
"He can't get better?" "The doctor says he can't,
but he just might stay like this, week after week."
For what? I wondered.
It was cooler on the porch.
My moment of dozing had brought me hard awake.
Moonlight shimmered all over a wet meadow,
but the mosquitoes won. I went to bed
wondering if my father had forgiven

my first-hand self for not being his second-hand image.
Did he suppose, if I hadn't gone to sea,
hadn't come home to scribble and teach the young
after a fashion, we two could have averted
that debtor's pyramid of second mortgages,
of loans to pay the interest on loans?
All that was left of too much was this little,
this farmhouse bought with a pittance of my mother's
before he was helped from the court, incredulous,
a bankrupt, under a deficiency judgment.
Shelter, at least, until they took it for taxes.

The student punched me awake. "He's asking for you."

The eyes, more watery blue than I remembered,
wandered until they found me, a yard distant.
"Something I want you to do, " my father mumbled.
Taking his unfleshed fingers, I was startled
by their desperate grip. There were long pauses
as he told me where he had left his fishing rod,
and which was the garden corner best for worms.
"They're feeding me on pap," he objected, hoarsely.
"I want you to get me some trout for my breakfast.
Never–failing–trout stream–" Asleep again.
Echo of the advertisement that had hooked them.
"Never-failing trout stream on the property."
A trickle so narrow that the grass closed over it.
On earlier visits I had found him there
drowsing, pole in hand, the barb of his hook
hidden still in its original worm.
My mother said he had never caught a killy.
Remembering the Raquette River, hard portages,
remembering the muskellunge, I wanted to weep.
"If you can't catch a trout with a worm, you're no fisherman,"
he used to say, back in that other world,
"and if you use a worm, you're no fisherman either."

But he was too impetuous to whip a fly.
He was a troller, a plug fisherman,
loving the reel's whir till the long cast settled
a hundred yards away by the pickerel weed.

I found the rod. My mother woke. I told her.
She sat by the bed while the student had his breakfast.
"You're not going to do it?" "I've got to try."
"There never were any trout, and you both know it."
I did not urge it as a kind of penance.
She understood. There was always that between us.

Night crawlers lay flat under the weeds
on the wet garden. I took a few and started
downhill through soaking grass, slapping black flies.
Beyond the first stone wall, what I had known
as a foot-wide trickle was a spilling torrent
from the long rains. Black flies, scouting in squadrons,
got the tang of my sweat, came storming.
Under low branches, I baited the hook,
tried not to scratch. I could feel my face swelling.
The worm swept to the surface. I gave it line,
waited—until, digging at my tormenters,
I saw their crushed bodies clogged under my nails.
My hand dangled and came up wearing leeches.
Convulsed, I let them suck, aware of the counsel:
Don't panic and tear them. Use a cigarette.
More leeches waved on the long wet grass.
When is the end of penance? The rod twitched,
stiffened. I played it lightly, without hope.
A fish. A trout, too trivial to be legal.
Had it fought upstream? I snapped its neck, baited
the hook again, hit flies. A long wait later—
a minute or an hour—and once more
the line shivered. Numerical fulfillment:
trout, plural, for his breakfast—if my father

could swim up somehow from his own long dark
to have at least a whiff and a glimpse of them.

When I came in my mother cried her horror.
The mirror showed me why. As I burned off
my blood-fat leeches she prepared a compress.
"Idiot!" she said. I took the trout from my pocket.
She stared at them and me as if frightened.
"You really caught them?" "Yes." Then she was weeping
I tried to comfort her, but this was release
from a long discipline made in New England.
"I prayed that you would catch them. Look what it cost you."

A sound from the bed: my father trying to speak.

"Show me—my trout." I put them in his hand,
small and slimy. As the fingers closed
the student moved to snatch them. Then, with an odd
explosion of his breath, he backed away.
My father's eyes seemed to have suddenly cleared.
"I want you to fry them for me, " he whispered, "in butter,
with the heads on." My mother almost laughed
and I knew why. When had there been butter?
"Even if he could eat," she said, "the doctor
told me, 'No fried food,' oh, months ago."
"Maybe the smell would please him?" "Yes, maybe it would.
Wait, I know what." She came back from the kitchen
shaking a Mason jar with some top milk in it.
We spelled each other till the butter formed,
enough, a teaspoonful. His nostrils quivered
to the smell of fried trout, drifting from the kitchen.

She brought them on a plate with sprigs of parsley,
no fork, no knife, and set them on a chair
by the bedside. His lids flickered. He was waking.
The movement that had taken all my strength

yesterday afternoon, he made by himself:
turned on his side. As he reached toward the trout
the student tried to stop him, but I was there first.
My father took a fish by its crisp tail,
fell back on the bed, smiled, and slowly
put the head between his teeth—and chewed.
"I can't let him," the student said. "Why not?"
"He'll choke to death," and then he shrugged, *what difference?*
My mother, breathless, did not interfere
as she saw him crunch the trout again, through the backbone.
Third bite, fourth, fifth, and it was gone—
head, bones, tail and all, all swallowed.

He was sleeping quietly when the doctor came.
Until the tests were made we admitted nothing.
He looked up, puzzled. "What the devil! He's stronger."
When I confessed, he wobbled his jowls at me.
"Give him the other for supper if he wants it."
He did. We gave it to him. He slept well.

With my head tied in netting, and gloves on,
I tried again the next day and the next.
The trout were a non-recurring miracle.
On the fourth day the doctor scowled and said,
"You've got a job?" "Half time," I admitted.
"Better go back and see if its still yours.
I'll give you a ring again when we need you."

The next time I saw my father he was riding a horse.

The Horses

Rather then let some Nazi get the only
job that offered, I worked my way across
in the S.S. *Bremen*, autumn of '34.
The cablegram caught up with me in London:
FATHER DIED TODAY DONT COME MOTHER

In my furnished-room-with-breakfast I sat watching
an old man steer his dog around the iron
fence of Brunswick Square, vanishing
into a pea souper of acrid fog
to emerge at the opposite side. Someone later
described him as having a back like a Hansom cab.
He called to mind my favorite tropic pastime—
guessing at a dolphin's reappearance
from the slope of his dive, and never guessing right—
with the difference that these emergences
were all foreseeable. Impulse pulled me
down to pace beside him. He nodded. We walked,
listening to the far clop clop of hooves
from the only sensible transport for such weather.
Horses knew where they were in the yellow murk.

At last he spoke. "You'll have a spot of tea?"
I'd finished breakfast, tea and all, a horror
to a coffee drinker, but one I had to get used to.
"You're an American." "And you're Irish."
His laugh was the crash of a wave. Over the teacups
he looked through heavy lenses as my fingers
curled the curt message to a cylinder.
"Bad news, I expect."
"Yes."
My problem spilled:
Should I go down to the Isle of Dogs, hunting
another ship to work my way back home in—
too late for the funeral? I described my father
seated restless at his roll-top desk

as if his knees were gripping saddle leather
while his spirit cantered the sweep of opal beaches
he never had seen, in the Spice Islands,
sniffing out turmeric, cinnamon—
or galloped down the Coromandel Coast
seeking plumbago headed up in barrels
with carved elephants added for good measure.
Elephants marched along the farmhouse mantel,
teak and plumbago, balancing their howdahs
under framed pictures of my father's horses,
most of them posed in the ring at Durland's.

"Don't go to his body," my new friend counseled.
"Follow his spirit. That's what you'd intended?"
For the first time, then, I saw his shelves—
poetry—poetry—poetry.
Next day I came to thank him with the diffident,
inevitable gift: my own first clutch of verses.
He reached for a book of his, *Deirdre, A Drama*
in Three Acts, and entered an inscription:
"Go East, young man / A.E."
That was the onset
of an odd voyage. At my publisher's club
a fellow guest whose name I should have known,
but did not, scribbled me a cryptic chit
to take to the P & O in Leadenhall Street.
It got me—not the best I had dared hope for,
a berth as a deck hand—but instead a startling
passage to Singapore in the First Class
at the "victualling rate," ten shillings a day,
vestige of an old *noblesse oblige*
that lingered for the lucky. I was lucky,
with just enough left over to tip the stewards.
The problem of staying alive at the ends of the earth
after such luxury was for later solving.

Across a sea like broken antimony

a horseman waved and waved from Cape Spartel,
too far for recognition, as the *Ranchi*
coasted to Tangier. Nearing Marseilles,
a harbor made with hands, I watched a rider
rein his horse high on a seawall.
At Malta, Suez, Aden, a horseman loomed.

Bogus catharsis! But when Africa
pulled Bab al Mandab down over the slope
of ocean, till a ship's rail was the inner
edge of distance that had no outer edge,
I stood at the taffarel, where the log line ticked,
and did what I could to reel in the past.

Beyond the spandrel always left agape
between our generations, what had made
son and father, like magnetic positives,
repellent in their similarity—
until an auctioneer's impersonal hammer
struck in two pieces the harmonious centaur,
tearing firm ligatures of love that gripped him
for fifteen years to his ultimate horse, Chester?
Could nothing less than this have bound a son
to the torn side of his father? Had we been parted
by something as agreeable as truth?
Even in childhood I had grown uneasy
over the anecdotes that never wilted
for want of elaborations, to be retold
next time as if they had been there always.
I wondered if every story had begun
with no more truth than there seemed in its new details.

Athwart the Great Nicobar, days later,
watching multitudinous rags of cloud
eclipse the running stars in a monsoon night,
I rehearsed a story of his: the horse banquet,
held—as he made a point of it to tell

new listeners—before I was thought of.
Thirty gentlemen saddled up at Durland's,
angled the park to Fifth, at 59th,
posted to 44th Street as a squadron,
where they dined on horseback at Louis Sherry's.
Heard first in miniature, it seemed unlikely.
Embellishment soon pushed it to fantasy.
Two by two, guests on their horses soared
in the freight elevator to the fourth storey
where Sherry's largest room was layered in sawdust.
There were special trays, shaped to the mounts' withers.
Opera hatted horsemen—in boiled shirts
and dinner jackets, over whipcord breeches—
ate cherrystone clams, turtle soup, lobster Newburg,
grouse, venison, Napoleons, Camembert,
all the while sipping Mumm's Extra Dry
through tubes from bottles in iced saddle bags.
Waiters, in tails as usual, served the riders.
Waiters disguised as grooms brought for the horses
feedbags of imported oats, from Scotland.
They had shovels and scuttles to cope with the outcome.
The gentlemen rode back in column of fours
for a last inverse stirrup cup at Durland's—
'48 Otard—and so to bed.

Rather than hear it told again, again,
I would hurry down to my basement cave, sulfuric
with verity. Reagents, measured out
in milligrams and cubic centimeters,
fizzed sweetly in the Erlenmeyer flask
to exact results foretold in the manual.
My reliable world of Bunsen burner truths
crumpled on the day when I confronted
Pilate's sudden question. What became
of the truth of chemistry when science pimped
for avarice? What had my truth become?

A loop of words, speared with the nib of a pen
from the bone flask where the mind bubbles?
Truth revealed in a quick shiver
along my spine? If that could be the test—
and it was the test—I took my truth on faith.

Stars moved from cloud to cloud with the long roll
of the *Ranchi*. As she spread her wings
of glittering protozoa, I learned a truth:
that water burns, that every breaking wave
can lift a plume of fire. By flickering sealight
I saw that my father's art was speech perfectible.
Our truths were hostile, but our truth was one.

When we came to the country of my father's ghost,
from coral battlements of the old fort
guarding Pulo Pinang, I scanned the shore—
but every horseman on the long parade,
as he posted nearer, waned to an Englishman.

Weeks followed on the beach at Singapore.
Infant typhoons, like supple dervishes,
plagued the poor fishermen. I wrote a little
in the *Malaya Times*, till I found a ship
for Hong Kong. Not by the shortest line
I made it home, after a year or so,
to drain from my hollow bones the tropic heat
in a farmhouse winter, breaking ice for water,
chopping wood by the cord, writing the book
made truer by invention. Elephants clumped
the mantel, under photographs of horses,
each with elaborate stories to evoke.

Except for Chester, I best remembered Scout.
It was from Scout, at Durland's, that my father
swung me to a pure white horse with a tail

that touched the tanbark, set my narrow back
against a big man's hard-as-hickory belly.
After a turn of the ring my father said,
"You can tell them, when you go to school next year,
that you rode with Buffalo Bill." It was Buffalo Bill,
a carbine in the socket at his knee,
ready to lead a parade to Madison Square.
With the intrepid candor of a child
I asked him why he wore his hair like a girl's.
He said, to keep the rain out of his collar.

On a spring day, when the book was almost done,
a letter came. "I think I've seen a picture
of your father, in this week's *Life.*"
My mother borrowed a copy from a friend.
The caption read, "The $50,000
Horse Banquet." Thirty riders sat
in a great curve on horses with broad trays
affixed to their withers. The fifth from the left
was holding a tube to his lips that led to a bottle.
His hand hid part of a face that seemed to be
the face of my father, sitting his high horse
under the chandeliers of Louis Sherry's.

•3•

The Good Treason

Iron Mirror

We make our enemy in the image of our fear.
What courage might have made us, who can guess?
Beyond this blinding metal, see how clear
the devil stands, shaped to our inwardness.

High Suttee/3 November 1957–14 April 1958

Laika, small bride of science,
hurled to the loneliest death,
through these tense days we wait
your portent: bright parabola.

Flame down, skeletal meteor.
Roar from the alien waste
burning
into your own sweet air
to snap the long suspension of our guilt.

Bright Heraclitus

As their dark circle tightened on the rim
we closed our whirling ranks.
Eastern horns
belched in the north, in the west.
From groin and glottis of our sudden dead
we tore unvarying arrows.
Horn bray, bow twang,
loud in the south now,
riding hoof-struck thunder.

Order—keep order—
by order from the center.

And then it happened: your straight lunge of thought,
axial, ardent, not centrifugal.
Breaking their studded ring
woven of flesh in iron
out to an endlessness of raw stars rising
you thrust our vital anarchy: the mind.
Beyond their circle, nine transparent spheres
splintered. You broke the first.
Then, gladly, each of us
took his own way
to open the ringing sky.

Know-How

"Can do! Can do!" With whir and clunk
and very little getting drunk
they rinsed the mock-up in the oil.
They brought the cadmium to a boil,
then shoveled in with plop and plink
a hail of little hunks of zinc.
From blueprints like an iris petal
they dug the troughs to pour the metal,
and gave it flanges, whorls, and tapers
by snarling it through lathes and shapers.
Oh exquisite beyond applause
the curls that grew from carbide claws!
They whanged the rivets round the rims
while subcontractors milled the shims.
A vast conveyor belt conveyed
the marvel they had all but made
till there it stood—a lovely mass
of chromium and plexiglass.

Unautomated, came the buzz
of someone asking what it was.
They beat the pagan to his knees
and briskly cried, "Next order, please!"

1952-1958

The Good Treason

"We must have a new dictionary,
and the definition of this
much abused word must be:
'Treason, the rope by which the
real traitors seek to hang
those who resist them.'"
—Thomas Wentworth Higginson, 1856

And you, forging these bars for your own cage
to shut out un-America, what can you know
of my large country? Listen—

Once, in a school pageant, when I was a child,
on blistering Split Rock Road, I was Nathan Hale.
I stood in Nathan's very own hempen collar
(all ropes being one rope to the cry of SPY).
The scratch of his good treason ringed my throat.
Thank you, my country,
for the turncoat schoolmaster
who instructed me in the fiber of this devotion
when he did your dirty work as you were born.

No thanks for Benedict Arnold. None
for his closed parenthesis of double treason
scrawled like a broken cipher on your first page—

but for all your earliest, your irrepressible
printers, thank you—
for wild Matt Lyon, jailed when he shot small pica
at a president's regal britches.
Thanks especially
for your raffish Green Mountaineers
who straightaway voted their seditious Lyon
back into Congress
out of his freezing jail—

and also for your Harvard clergyman
Tom Higginson,
accessory before the fact of treason,
humming a hymn,
cuddling his new Sharp's rifle,
breaking your evil laws,
preaching dissension across murderous Kanzas,
his saddlebags fat with gold for slavery's murderer,
vast John Brown.

Thank you, on the balance, for John Brown—

and even more for the Conscience Whig,
Charles Sumner,
remote child of the immaculate virgin, Antigone—
Sumner, who stared through Webster's murky bargain
straight to the higher law.

No thanks (perhaps a pardon) for Black Dan.

No thanks (despite your pardon) for Robert E. Lee,
who took his oath to defend you,
took your instruction, high above the Hudson,
took your pay,
and turned to lunge so courteously at your heart.

Your man? Your best gray symbol?
Did you not know?
It is only the kind cause, ever,
makes the good treason.

Great Society

Worms drive their swirling tunnels, walled with spit,
beneath the level nation of the moles.
To whom is jetting man subordinate?
Trailed vapor drifts above the templed owls.

"Let man be his own least."

Strict as the crafty hornet, man has wrought
shelters for swarming, of his denser brick.
Shall nothing rake him with five-needled fright
in pads of panic lunging at his back?

"Let men be his own beast."

He crushes all. Who drags him to the ground
after the sudden lunge, the hopeless spurt –
tears a red branchwork lace of tubes, to grind
bicuspid on the hot, bunch-muscle heart?

"Let man be his own feast."

1952–1972

Parley in the Middle Ground

"Make peace! Our tenuous battle draws
twang-thin across a burnt, blown world.
Your final weapon, crazed with flaws,
shatters against this trivial shield."

Ultimate weariness came down:
could any terms invert our deeds?
He tried us: *"Keep this crumbling town.*
Only—give back my renegades."

We felt the acid instant burn—
but who were we to be disposers?
Without his prompting we could learn
ways of our own to end as losers.

He shrugged in confidence that we
must soon return for grimmer handling.
We stood against the wind, to see
his glowing hocks in the dark dwindling.

1952-1969

Lines for an Inauguration / 20 January 1973

We are the new gods,
the Americans.
Lords of the earth and air
we make what we please.

The old Space Walkers,
merciful, merciless,
lounged in the sky.

Grasping their strength,
scorning their weakness,
their mercy,
we have driven them out.

We can do what we please.
It has pleased us to hunt
Diana the Huntress
from her high home.

As we stepped from the void,
Moon Walkers,
we saw no sign of her.
The Huntress had fled.

It has pleased us to kill
imagination.
We have made a cold cinder
of the warm Moon.

Lest we hesitate
before the unimaginable,
we have killed sin.

We, the harsh gods,
the Americans,
sullen, cruel, vindictive,

can make what we please.

It has pleased us to make
Richard Nixon
in our own image
to reach round the bending earth
under the cold Moon
and send children running
prettily aflame.

•4•

Memory, Quick Dolphin

Original Sin

I remember now how first I knew what death was.
I remember the air rifle, the Daisy pump gun,
smelling of 3-in-One oil, and stiff in action.
Fire at random. Fire at a flying crow.
Aim at his wicked beak. While the bullet flies,
the heart of the crow will fly to where the beak was.

Fire at a perch in water, but remember
how the oar bends along the line of sight,
making a sliding joint upon the surface.
Remember that, and aim below the perch.
Fire at a tin can, which the BB shot
can puncture if the muzzle of the air gun
is almost touching. Fire at a stone, sharp angled,
and hear the tsing, the ricochet, the whining
snip of the torn bullet, tearing oak leaves.

Do not fire at a chipmunk, or a pigeon.
Fire at a crow, fire at an English sparrow.
Use up the little money rolls of shot.
Fire at the sharp rat-noses in the gaps
under the chicken coop. Life dodges quickly.

And then the day came when I knew what death was—
the day when life, intent on feather-preening,
was late in lunging upward from the twig.

Warm in the hand, its flight forever ended,
death was a fallen sparrow, with chipmunk markings,
and a small blue bubble of lead under the skin.

1943–1948

Man in the Street: Mexico

spilt wreckage   bones
   in a little flesh
      in a sprawl of rags
dark long hair like a broken
   fan in the dust   people
carefully sightless
   passing

we stood
   we stared their eyes
      toward knees drawn up
at the angle of endless hunger
   our eyes stabbed theirs
      for a reason
got no reason   their
   calm eyes glanced
      at rattling fronds
at a white mirage   volcano

past   long past
   but memory aches anew
      at your quick cry
as you touched the parchment
   forehead
      was it fever
and pressed the useless
   pesos into his hand

1951-1973

Candace

> "Clothes: she spent her
> most meaningful moments
> not wearing any."
> —Ramon Guthrie
>
> in *Black Squirrels and*
> *Albert Einstein*

Candace came at me, not because I was me—
though I still was, till midway
of a humid afternoon—
but because Pualani,
fresh from playing front-and-center
in the Hula line at the Royal Hawaiian
(O beautiful for spacious thighs
for amber waves of groin)
was being as amiable to me
as she would have been to anybody
and therefore must be displaced.

Great-great-granddaughter of first come,
first served missionaries,
Candace adored native Hawaiians—
if they were male,
which Pualani abundantly
wasn't. The okolehao went round
and round, until I did too.

My next awareness
was of water, cascading down
my brow—and there was Candace
in another part of the waterfall,
giggling, wearing only water.
Very becoming. She led me
out of the downpour to our clothes,
festooning a dwarf papaya.

I was harder to undress, she said,
than her kid brother, aged three,
who never would go to bed.
I would, I told her. She giggled again
and eclipsed with her halter
her considerable protuberances,
if I may borrow an apt phrase
from an inapt source, Dr. Samuel
Johnson, who employed it
in another connection.

My head, not at the time level,
was teeming with ideas
as she drove us from Sacred Falls
over the Pali, in twilight,
back toward Honolulu—where, as it turned out.
she had a date.

Next morning I was sleeping it off
when a middle-sized porpoise hit me:
Candace, bouncing
in a friendly, small-girl fashion,
on my chest, mostly,
in her wet bathing suit.
"We've been swimming all night," she said,
"every place we could think of,
but just as I got Timmy into his pyjamas,
I remembered we'd missed the Halekulani."

So we swam at the Halekulani,
she whizzing through the water
with her easy crawl—taught her
by the great Sheriff Kahanamoku himself—
while I flippered in her wake.
We had okolehao Manhattans for breakfast
on the lanai of the Moana, until she yawned

and decided it was time to go to bed.
High time, I agreed, but she meant
to bed to sleep.

Off and on, all summer, it was like that.
Nothing came of it, not in my case anyhow.
Considering the novel ways in which
it seemed never quite to happen
I began to wonder if Candace
fulfilled her menehune tumescence
wholly by shucking her clothes.

One last grace note. After we'd drifted
apart from a never achieved
nearness we fetched up by separate routes
knee to knee at an impromptu
Makiki Heights strip poker game.
Across the table the new face
was that of Lieutenant St. Lawrence,
just in by pig boat at Pearl Harbor
from his obviously only prior tour
of duty, at the Boston Navy Yard.
With exquisite discipline the lieutenant
(j.g.) kept his eyes aimed point blank
at the spots on his cards.
Candace, giggling, hardly glanced at hers.
He played it cool—cool as a ramrod in a high
white collar can, midway of a Hawaiian
September—threw in each
dubious hand, didn't strip off
so much as a white glove all evening.
Candace lost with an inspired
attention to the fine points of losing.

At last the lieutenant's eyes began to sidle
from overclad royal persons in his hands

toward his least clad opponent. Even so,
in the superb tradition of the service,
he starched his upper lip, and managed to hold
her selectively tanned
torso just at the edge of the outer
orb of vision—until
with a squirm and a lurch beside me
she freed herself from an ultimate ounce or two
of fabric which, in the likewise admirable
orthodox tradition of strip poker,
was (or were) her panties—flipped them across
to the victorious j.g. He,
hooking them out of the air with a sudden aplomb
that I have never ceased admiring, shuffled
the cards expertly, stared at her and said,
"Your deal, Miss Arkwright—ah,
may I call you Candace?"

Memory, Quick Dolphin

Herodotus says that Arion, cast overboard in the Aegean, was carried home to Athens on a friendly dolphin's back.

1.

Caught in binoculars, that hummingbird's head,
glitter of green and ruby, is a hypodermic
needle, probing the vulvas of delphinium:
reason enough for memory's dolphin-shuttle—
lost, seen, diving to resurface
through the fluid skin of time—back to the day
when two Prohibitions ended. Rheingold beer
glowing in legal bottles at Gristede's,
first and lesser wonder, after long waiting.
Your Boston Bull, half as impatient as I was,
hauling your wrist straight out toward Gracie Square.

2.

This phallus of blue dolphins under my window
looses an emissary of remembrance:
beer down, shades up, letting in a mixture
of street light and moonlight to draw double shadows.
Your foolish dog, snuffling a bleak dislike
of your strange visitor—and that was mutual.
You, my indolent calyx, whispering flower,
barred with soft light, a tigress suddenly.
I, spent dolphin, settling to depths of sleep
beneath the tingle of your wandering fingers.
Dolphin awakened. Again? Oh, yes, again.

3.

Blue, green, ruby, hummingbird among dolphins,
were there two later nights, or three? And then?
We never spoke of marriage. We went on
into our separate marriages. Only one letter,

years later, and one meeting—later still.
You, my slim calyx, heavy with middle age.

4.

After the unexplainable cuts the event,
never go back, except on the back of a dolphin.
Now this blue phallus, blurring time through lenses,
weaves in a wind, jostling your Boston Bull,
who chose, on the last night, his perfected moment
to sink deft fangs into my bare right heel.

Condottiere

His bulging codpiece, with its gypsum bows
five hundred years hard-knotted (what a pity!)
is soft in twilight, if a trifle gritty,
like the braided muscles in their stony hose.
Somewhat by giving, more by dodging, blows
he lived. His adequate sonnets lured the pretty,
practical ladies of each taken city
before time chipped his arrogant Tuscan nose.

Diminished now, in evening's shadowy farewell,
he hints at nothing of the last disaster.
Stone's firmer stuff than ulcered meat to wear well.
Oh, he was brisk, but the Black Death pricked faster.
Half a millennium now, beneath this stairwell,
he's stretched a tryst in pitted alabaster.

Autumn in the Fun House

At a rumpled mirror she brakes him to a halt.
                    Kneecaps ajerk
from scared leg-bracing in the roller coaster
he contemplates a spindle-shank buffoon
depaunched by optic quackery.

Be somebody else. Never be who you are.
                    Back in the green season
we all went wavering sooner or later sidewise
in the mirror behind the bottles behind the bar.
How long does it take to learn what's wrong with mirrors?

Speeding against loss she steers for another
                    glass-and-mercury swindle.
The juke box yammers. He stares at it unnerved.

Designed on purpose to sound like that. Of course.
                    But to look like that
act of choice—deliberate! O my god!

Her pleading fingers tug him past a chaos
                    of slamming bumper cars.
"Kiss me." He kisses her. "Why won't you ever
say it? Say, 'I love you.'" The cars crash.

She drags him toward the fish pond, hoping still
                    to haul up cardboard love
hooked on the little bent pins of rebuke.

•5•

Brant Point

David Today

Your blood runs muddled,
my polyglot,
from Dutch and English
and Welsh and Scot;
but to honor you
in this year of shame,
we have named you David,
a Jewish name.
Upon your hand—
a scant inch long—
we lay the sense
of your brother's wrong.
To this frail case
of gristle and skin
we trust the fortunes
of all your kin—
your Negro brother,
your brother the Jew—
of all who suffer
from being few.

In cruel times
for a child to share
your mother has dropped you,
well aware
that flesh must carry
the mind's high stake,
since the world we have
is the world we make.

Let nothing rob you
of discontent.
Your thin, first protest
was early spent—
a cradle tempest,
not loud, not long—

but your puny anger
will yet be strong;
and we bid you nurse it,
while we nurse you,
to turn on Gentiles
who hate the Jew,
on gentlemen
who in pride of race
would burn black problems
they dare not face.

Poor and lucky,
we can ill afford
a silver spoon
or a silver cord;
but your name is David—
we bring you, instead,
one smooth flat stone
from the clean brook bed,
and with this for birthright
may you, at length,
have little of comfort,
much of strength.
We could wish you homeless
under a ledge
with a mind that burns
through the skull's thin edge—
better so,
in the sleety rain,
than plump and cozy
in belly and brain.

For there's work to be done
and all's not well.
The giants we fostered
are yours to fell.

The peace we squandered
is yours to win,
by anger flashed outward
and hate held in.
Let these be single
when each is great:
anger blown clear
of the coals of hate—
keep hate for ideas,
anger for men,
now the fools of evil
are loose again.

And when metals cancel
and wits lock fast,
one smooth flat stone
can win, at the last,
through fear and the will
to master fear
with the sling of David.

The giants are here.

1940–1941

Parents, Beware

This is the beautiful world of Choco-Pops.
ZOOM! Through the asteroids Green Lantern plunges
past Goofy, and the Pepsi-Cola cops
clinging blunt-fingered to their rocket's flanges.

Here the lost ends of space are slid together,
and shrill young voices call, planet to planet.
Here the caped hero dares the airless weather,
circling to Saturn's ring, to sit upon it.

Evil's astir. One phoenix-word, "Shazam!"
flames Billy Batson into Captain Marvel.
The wall-brick scatters at his plunge, and WHAM!
A soggy villain SPLATS upon the gravel.

Sweet non-Copernican, near-Ptolemaic
universe, blown out of box-top wishes,
tangle of Futuramic and archaic,
where brontosaurus falls as the death ray flashes,

whose are its values? Which absurd child flings us
a solace for our dream of order, broken?
What wild astronomy is this, that brings us
the new world Krypton, seen in a pan of Flakorn?

Moral, foreshortened, slam-bang sky and earth,
does it reveal a draftsman, or his clients?
The best of it is theirs—belief and mirth—
but was it children who procured these giants?

Grant us one world, Geographer. But where's
our true choice, as the edge of reason crinkles:
that hoof-hacked, Silver-shaken globe of theirs?
This ball of poisoned motes that grips our ankles?

Of my son's oaten hero, shall I say
the mind-made word that mocks the spirit's hunger?
Young skies will empty, splendor drain away.
Hurry and mail the box top! Address LONE RANGER.

A postman, peering through wide Western air,
will know him by his mask, his silver bullet.
Well, who rides firmer earth? Parents, beware!
There's plenty of time for truth, if you can tell it.

1949–1950

Brant Point

For David

Vessels making for Nantucket harbor
along the Dionis coast should
"keep as much as a cable's length
from the shore at Brant-point
until the light-house bears S.S.W."
then "haul for the point, to avoid
the *Coetue*-flats."
—Captain Lawrence Furlong, 1800

Sunset

High gulls flick late copper.
At our backs a siren grieves,
a bell's lip shakes the air.
Peripheral bongs return
coned from a front of fog above Coetue—
thin cliff for echoes.
Water's chilly ghost at turn of tide
outflanks a ghosting yawl.
We on the sand
feel the quick plummet of her anchor rode
for one last grip upon a slipping world.
She veers in space.
The foul tide sweeps to sea.

Nightfall

Toeing grooved sand, you turn
as vermilion light blooms on its heavy stem.
Nantucket, sloping town,
slides under moted water.
Night takes us both
now, in the first condition—
wet sand, wet salt, wet air,

in a dish of nothing
covered by blunted light.

From the yawl's clock, four double chimes

A rippled, restive dust of rock and shell
wanders and regathers
to keep the old shape of this elbowed foreland
where the tide runs sidewise.

Is this the edge of the hour
for your long stride,
shoreward or seaward?

Poised on a rim of choice
you should find sea-marks—
and there are no sea-marks.
The light is blotted by the stippled air
that braids a gust of bird cries.
Quick, plunging brightness pelts the target lens
from upper freedom
and the cries are still.
Scoop for your thigh life's half-grave in the sand
for the short death of sleep.

Midnight

The yawl's horn brays.
You stir. (Is this the hour?)
Hand seeking hand, we rise together.
Under our heels the fierce and laboring sun
swings in deep ether.
Huge world, broken small,
heave at our wrists,
force this one more division.

Father of words
that spill too late,
too soon,
how shall instruction deepen into counsel?

Childhood flung backward,
you have taken your night stance
in a sidling tug of the sea.
My hand hangs broken.
Nothing is known.
Direction warps and wanders.
The gurgle at your knees,
the jetty bell,
the yawl's horn,
lose their way
in the dragged cerements of a colder mist.
Moments ago a four-knot current
gave you the lie of the parental shore.
Now, off a coast unsure as Lilliput's,
you are self-stripped
even of that thin guidance
as the still tide again
pivots, turning.

Tear from my eyes the bodkins of this dark!

Water, reversing,
whispers at your knees.
I wait, unworded.

The yawl's clock strikes two bells

Choice guides you to my shoulder
in the vibrant night
in your own time.

II

> "When you near the shoal you will
> have very light colored water,
> together with white and black sand
> and pieces of green shells."
> —Furlong

Midwatch

Sleep.
Have I given you anything, ever,
but the harsh burden, love,
and half of shape?
Hiked out to wind'ard on a humming gun'le,
I gave you tiller fingers—
flat sheet, muscular to the hurrying squalls—
drench of joy—
yesterdays together.

In the waist of the watch glass
I would stop the sand,
remembering.

You were a stranger in the dark caul.
Sudden love shook me when you were born.

Where is wisdom?
Now is tomorrow.
Sleep.

Three bells

By your own impulse
you will learn

alone
the use of danger.
Rightful as Gulliver
you will seek the wild shores.

Four bells

Beyond the red nun, where a fingered shoal
points the rip westward,
who puts breath to horn?
Sleep, as I dream the occurrence
into your dream.

He is not lost.
Counseled by Furlong,
he sends his curious line
(ragtagged and knotted with the marks and deeps)
down from the forechains
through black nightwater
till its questing tallow in a snout of lead
nuzzles the undermap.
It fetches up
a starry freckle of quahaug shell
scoured to the size of buckshot.
By this,
in the blind, loud, undirectional fog,
he knows he is off Dionis.
He is sure of his ground.
The sand accepts his flukes beyond Whale Rock.

Son, do I pierce your dreaming?

Five bells

When a ceaseless flow and ebb of the easily seen
beguiles the leaders
who take swift bearings from the merely visible,
what holding ground will grip
the hard hook of your truth?
When fog eats outline,
when a foul tide of rumor sweeps good men
to whirl them all one way,
may your bare heels
serve for ground tackle
in the worse while that follows.

Dig in.

May your truth hold.

Daybreak

Fog bunches skyward in the brails of light,
clearing a rake of spars.
The yawl, her hook apeak, sets jib and jigger.
Her stays all gold,
she rides the sun-dance east to Monomoy.

Turn, son, from that delight
and gather with me for sand burial
the sacrifices of ferocious man
to Pharos, for our safety on the sea—
under the lighthouse stalk its fallen petals,
these shattered birds.

We kneel at graveside in our new estate—
equal sharers of the gain and guilt,
near and lost,
held by one spidery cable—
love only,
only love.

Six bells

Half in blue morning,
half in the sea's green night,
you lean again
on the hard tide.
Beyond your striving ribs
I see the bobble of Lilliputian masts
furring safe harbor.

Now is tomorrow.

How soon,
in what tempestuous new tomorrow,
will the loud rip of sure opinion whelm
the strong horn
of your unwanted warning?
May you in truth stand then
as you stand now, Gulliver,
sand-braced at least,
wet-ankled,
as you tow the pygmies home
whatever the tide.

1955–1967